I0800661

FUN HANDBAGS

Schiffer Publishing Ltd®

4880 Lower Valley Road, Atglen, PA 19310 USA

FUN HANDBAGS

Schiffer Publishing, Ltd.

Cover:
Beige fabric tote trimmed with beige vinyl, with a vinyl strap and turn-lock clasp, double beige vinyl top handles, an oval wooden base and rooster appliqué in colorful, shiny sequins and rhinestones in shades of red, green, gold, pale blue, and mauve, opening to a single compartment with one open and one zippered pocket, lined with tan vinyl. 11.75 inches by 10.75 inches by 3.5 inches, 1950s. *Courtesy of Gemma Pomilio.* $95-105.

A Note About Prices

The price ranges given here are based on the current retail market for handbags in excellent condition. Prices may vary according to condition, quality of craftsmanship, label or designer, uniqueness of style, shopping venue, and trends in the marketplace.

Other Schiffer Books by Desire Smith:
Hats
Vintage Style
Fashionable Clothing from the Sears Catalogs, Early 1950s
Fashionable Clothing from the Sears Catalogs, Late 1960s
Fashionable Clothing from the Sears Catalogs, Early 1970s
Fashionable Footwear
Handbag Chic

Library of Congress Control Number: 2006921038

Designed by John P. Cheek
Cover design by Bruce Waters

Type set in Freestyle Script D/Dutch801 Rm BT

ISBN: 0-7643-2493-4
Printed in China
1 2 3 4

Published by Schiffer Publishing Ltd.
4880 Lower Valley Road
Atglen, PA 19310
Phone: (610) 593-1777; Fax: (610) 593-2002
E-mail: Info@schifferbooks.com

For the largest selection of fine reference books on this and related subjects, please visit our web site at **www.schifferbooks.com**
We are always looking for people to write books on new and related subjects. If you have an idea for a book please contact us at the above address.

This book may be purchased from the publisher.
Include $3.95 for shipping.
Please try your bookstore first.
You may write for a free catalog.

In Europe, Schiffer books are distributed by
Bushwood Books
6 Marksbury Ave.
Kew Gardens
Surrey TW9 4JF England
Phone: 44 (0) 20 8392-8585;
Fax: 44 (0) 20 8392-9876
E-mail: info@bushwoodbooks.co.uk
Website: www.bushwoodbooks.co.uk
Free postage in the U.K., Europe; air mail at cost.

Dedication

To my beautiful daughter-in-law, Erin Smith, who understands the fundamentals of vintage style—creativity and fun!

Acknowledgments

Sincere thanks to Peter and Nancy Schiffer for their creative approach to publishing, for their willingness to experiment with cover design, and for their confidence in me to provide content worthy of a great cover. Especially, thanks to Nancy Schiffer, my editor, the most gracious and patient person I know. I am deeply indebted to Jeffrey Snyder who did the wonderful photography for the book, and to John Cheek, who designed *Fun Handbags*, Bruce Waters, who designed the cover, and the members of the staff at Schiffer Publishing, who have been so very helpful.

Sincere thanks to my friends at Alderfer Auction Company, Hatfield, Pennsylvania: Sandy Alderfer, Vernon Martin, Wayne Mugrauer, Joyce Ruth, Charlie Moyer, Judy A. Moyer, George Wilmot, Tara Flynn, and others who offered encouragement and help.

I am deeply indebted to the following individuals: Robert Browne, who so kindly permitted us to photograph handbags from his extensive collection of 20th century clothing and accessories; Mary Efron, who contributed several fascinating handbags from her personal collection; Linda J. Munson, who contributed exceptional designer handbags from her collection; Gemma Pomilio, who contributed some of the most whimsical handbags I have seen; and my friends, Barry and Joann Slosberg of Barry S. Slosberg, Inc., Auctioneers/Appraisers, Philadelphia, Pennsylvania. I must also thank Clyde Harris, Elsie Hench, Robert Hilton, Grace Miller, Bill Murray, and Lisa Reid for their help.

Finally, I must thank my family for their encouragement—my husband, Bruce Smith; my son Matthew Smith and his wife, Erin, and their daughters, Savannah and Brooklyn; my son Michael as well as my canine companion, the little royal, Chase.

Preface

The next time someone asks you, "Is it fun yet?", don't bother rolling your eyes and looking slightly exasperated. Don't bother smiling that faint, tentative smile. Look them straight in the eyes and announce unequivocally, "It's been fun all along." That's sure to throw them off for a few seconds while you collect your thoughts and try to remember just what exactly *has* been fun lately. Collecting handbags…but, of course.

Collecting is the nice face we put on a little compulsive shopping, bordering on obsession. At a certain point we know we have crossed the line when we can't even remember how many red handbags we have, or for that matter, when we have actually *carried* a red handbag. Then there's the matter of shades of red.

One day we have to attend an occasion that requires accessories. We find the handbag first, but now there's the matter of the shoes…and the dress, unless maybe we try to get away with a little "slip dressing." We've got the dress that looks great with the handbag and the shoes, but what about the coat? Should we go tone-on-tone, or should we move into a completely different color of the spectrum? And, what about gloves?

The dirty little secret here is that *it* almost always starts with the handbag—not the shoes, not the dress, certainly not the coat. And, can we find a pair of gloves, which means two gloves that *exactly* match? So, finally we're standing in front of the mirror for a practice run of the entire outfit—handbag, shoes, dress, coat, and gloves, and we realize we haven't got a stitch of underwear on. Forget that the last sentence ended with a preposition. This is serious.

If a girl could possibly know early-on, let's say by the age of four, how important handbags are, and will be for the rest of her life, perhaps she could start collecting right away. That would cut down on some of the uncertainty in her future, especially when it comes to special occasion dressing.

Handbags are fun and this book was crafted with that thought in mind. However, we'd all be better off if we took fun more seriously. So, this is a book full of contradictions about handbags. They may be expensive or inexpensive, serious or whimsical, antique or not so old, classic or unconventional, traditional or trendy.

As one who loves fashion, I have to own up to a little compulsive shopping myself. When I'm shopping for vintage, even in my dreams, I look for the best. That is subjective, of course, because it is based on my judgment. It's about what I like, what I believe has intrinsic merit, what I believe will work for me. I also look for handbags that are in excellent condition, inside and out. That is less subjective. We all know that something that is ripped, stained, cracked, or otherwise damaged is not an appropriate choice for a handbag. Remember, collectors, we must maintain! Buying good quality in excellent condition is a statement of high self-esteem.

Little girls' handbags from the 1950s, including white lace umbrella-shaped, trimmed with yellow velvet ribbon and flowers; natural straw with colorful raffia appliqué in a butterfly motif; white plastic with a hand painted flamingo, and lettering, "Miami Beach, Fla." *Author's collection*. $35 – 55 each.

Contents

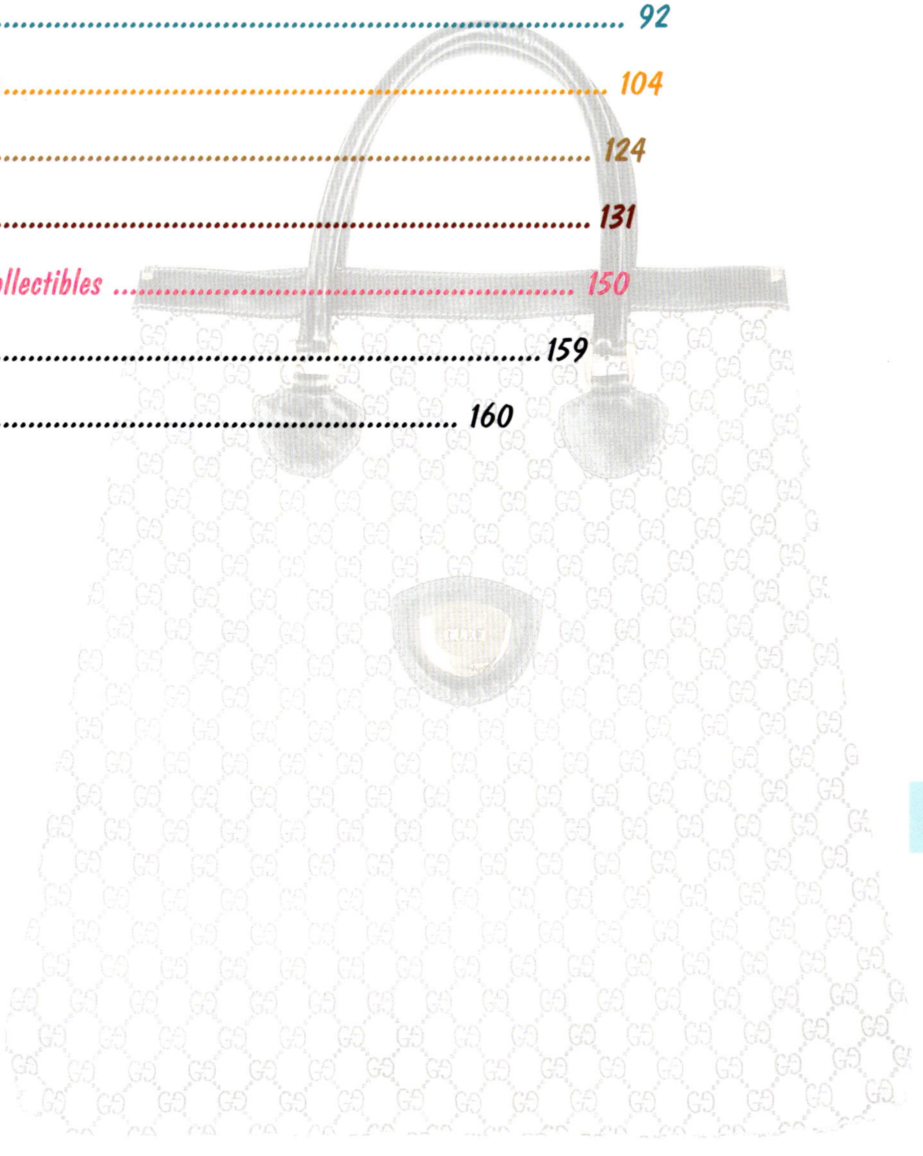

Introduction

Who has a crystal ball to look into the future of collectible handbags? We can only surmise, based on the past, that many handbags will be treasured and saved by their owners. Some will be given to children and grandchildren, or to other family members or friends; others will be sorted out when estates are dispersed, and perhaps some will be donated to charity or consigned to auction houses. Of the vast number of handbags now available in the marketplace, how can we determine which ones may be of significant value in the future? Which ones will be trendy and collectible? Which ones will be of interest to private collectors and curators of fashion museums?

Probably the biggest price jump has been made by the novelty totes of the 1950s. Many of these trendy handbags cost less than a dollar when first offered for sale. As a child I can remember seeing the now very collectible totes, with poodle dog appliqué, rhinestones, and sequins, lined up on the gondolas at F. W. Woolworth, with 89-cent price stamps. Some of these totes are now bringing well over three hundred dollars at auction.

Plastic handbags have significantly increased in value. These jewel-like box bags were never a dime-a-dozen, but many were priced very reasonably in the 1950s. Because so many have been chipped, crazed, clouded, or simply broken over time, handbags of this type in excellent condition are rare, and now command very high prices. One can expect to pay $375 - $650 for such a handbag in excellent condition. With embellishment, such as rhinestones, the price can be even higher.

Vintage designer handbags, such as Chanel, Mark Cross, Fendi, Gucci, Hermes, Judith Leiber, Pucci, and Louis Vuitton are important as collectible handbags, because of their fine craftsmanship. Dollar-for-dollar, it is impossible to say which designer handbag would be the best investment. Many of these handbags, especially those designed for daywear, have had considerable use before becoming available in the vintage marketplace. Generally the styles are classic, not trendy, which is not always advantageous in achieving collectible status. Designer handbags specifically for late day, special occasion, or evening use are more likely to increase in value, depending upon creativity of design and relative condition.

Women have been buying more handbags during the last decade. Accessories designers have been scraping the bottom of the pickle barrel, so to speak, to come up with new, creative designs. Everything has a name now. The more euphemistic "vagabond" bag has become the "hobo" bag. During the 1980s, everything had a monogram; designer logos were excruciatingly popular with the fashion elite. There is a current trend to revisit the monogram canvas, this time departing somewhat from the more traditional and classic styles.

I believe in mixing it up a little—inexpensive with expensive; trendy with classic. My fashion goal is to achieve a style of dressing which is creative, interesting, and yet affordable. I enjoy buying contemporary handbags that are different from any I have seen before, or if they take inspiration from an earlier style, they are providing a new dimension or interpretation of the earlier style. I believe that some of these unusual handbags will be the first in the collectibles line up, as time marches on. Who can know for sure, without that infallible crystal ball? But we should definitely take a chance, go with instinct, and by all means have fun!

Chapter One

All Business

The older I get, the more I'm convinced that nothing is all business. These handbags are getting real close though.

Brown alligator satchel style handbag, with decorative brown alligator straps, with gold-tone detailing, a brass clasp, single brown alligator top handle, with a single compartment, one zippered pocket, three open pockets, and a chestnut brown leather lining, gold-stamped *Mitch*. 10.5 inches by 7 inches by 5.5 inches, 1960s. *Courtesy of the Family of Bernice Harris*. $375 – 425.

Especially beautiful alligator and crocodile handbags from the 1950s and 1960s, have been on every collector's wish list for some time now. Buy a style that pleases you, and carefully evaluate the skins for condition issues, such as dryness and cracking. The good news is that these handbags were greatly prized by their original owners, and many are in excellent condition. If you must have Hermes, expect to pay a very high price.

White ostrich-embossed leather handbag, with a white ostrich-embossed leather-covered frame, gold-tone clasp, and single white ostrich-embossed leather top handle, with a single compartment, one open pocket, white faille lining, and white leather change purse, gold-stamped *Morris Moskowitz, MM, Genuine Leather*. 9 inches by 7.5 inches by 3.5 inches, 1960s. *Courtesy of the Family of Bernice Harris*. $145 – 165.

Handbags by Morris Moskowitz have been very interesting to collectors for some time. They are beautifully crafted with exquisite attention to detail.

Tan pigskin accordion handbag, with dark brown edging, a deep flap, gold-tone clasp, and double top handles, opening to three separate compartments, with three zippered pockets, one open pocket, and a beige leather lining. 11 inches by 8.5 inches by 2.5 inches, purchased at *Crouch & Fitzgerald* on Madison Avenue, NYC, early 1970s. *Courtesy of Linda J. Munson.* $375 – 425.

This handbag is beautifully crafted with great attention to detail. It has a classic, enduring style.

Tan double-*G* monogram canvas, trimmed with tan leather, with gold-tone double-*G* insignia, centered near the top, a zippered closure, and 21- inch shoulder strap, with a 5.25 inch by 1.5 inch shoulder pad, and a single compartment, lined with tan pigskin, with one zippered pocket. 11 inches by 8.5 inches by 2 inches, purchased at *Gucci*, Fifth Avenue, NYC, mid-1980s. *Courtesy of Linda J. Munson*. $275 – 325.

The signature canvas handbags, expensive status symbols of the 1980s, were all but obsolete during the 1990s, but in recent years have enjoyed a strong comeback.

Three lizard duffle bags, including dark green, burgundy, and tan, each with double lizard top handles, zippered closures, and leather linings, each with one compartment, three open pockets, and one zippered pocket. 9 inches by 7 inches by 5.5 inches, 1980s. *Courtesy of the Family of Bernice Harris*. $175 – 225 each.

There may be a lesson here: If you find a handbag that you really like, get it in every color.

Chapter Two

Past Pleasures

These handbags are keepers—memories of long ago and faraway.

Fine petit point handbag, with a still life motif on both sides, showing a floral bouquet on a table, in shades of ivory, green, burgundy, lavender, and rose, on a tan ground, with an embossed brass and silver frame, delicate chain handle, and unusual fold-over clasp, lined with gold silk, with a single compartment, a change purse, and two open pockets, edged in silver metallic, labeled *Morabito, Paris*. 10 inches by 8 inches by 1.25 inches, 1930s. *Courtesy of George Wilmot.* $575 – 650.

Everything about this handbag is incredible. The flowers are so beautifully executed in petit point that they appear to be real.

Fine petit point, with a different scene on each side, showing gates, buildings, incredible flowers, a fountain, ladies and gentlemen in period costume, classical sculpture and archways, in shades of green, tan, rose, lavender, gray, and black, on a pierced and engraved metal frame with sets and marcasite, lined with tan silk satin, with a single compartment and two open pockets, as well as a small change purse, attached with a chain, labeled *The Queen of Petit Point, Made In Vienna, Ges. Gesch. Studio, Maria Stransky, 2 Mariahilferstr.116, Vienna Austria.* 8 inches by 7 inches by 1.5 inches, 1930s. *Courtesy of George Wilmot*. $575 – 650.

This petit point figural and scenic bag raises the bar for its type. With incredible detail on both sides, fine workmanship and materials, this bag is a treasure.

Whiting & Davis hand painted metal mesh handbag, with a pastel floral design and the original paper hang tag intact. 5 inches by 8 inches, 1910-1915. *Courtesy of Mary Efron, NYC.* $575 – 625.

The pastel floral design is very unusual, as is finding such a handbag with its original hang tag.

White glass beaded handbag, with chain stitch embroidery in pastel shades of rose, green, gold, pale blue, and pink in an all over floral design, with a beaded and embroidered handle, gold-tone frame and clasp, and ivory satin lining with one compartment and two open pockets, labeled *Bags By Josef, Hand Beaded In France*. 10 inches by 7.5 inches by 1.5 inches, 1940s. *Courtesy of George Wilmot*. $250 – 275.

While the form is not particularly unusual, finding such a handbag in excellent condition is. The pastel shades tend to work well with a myriad of outfits for special occasions, such as weddings.

Special occasion purse, entirely beaded on both sides with round white glass beads, and diminutive clear glass bugle beads in a floral design, with a brass frame and hinged brass clasp, decorated with glass beads, also in a floral design, single round glass beaded top handle, with a single compartment, two open pockets, and a matching change purse, entirely lined with white silk. 9.5 inches by 7 inches by 1.5 inches, 1950s. *Courtesy of Erin Smith*. $125 – 175.

For all seasons and all times, this is a jewel.

Beaded bag with three examples of needle art: beading, appliqué, and embroidery. The scene shows a man smoking a large pipe, a woman in attendance, and a table with a flower. The frame is early Bakelite carved with a crouching dragon clasp, restored lining of yellow silk. 9 inches by 8.5 inches by 2 inches, 1910-1915. *Courtesy of Mary Efron, NYC*. $750 – 850.

An incredible handbag with an incredible frame!

Chapter Three

Retro Chic

Even though you're on a budget, you have an eye for putting a look together. Keep on it...before you know it, you'll be setting a trend.

Two-tone vinyl handbag in salmon pink and mandarin orange, with a single vinyl top handle, gold-tone frame and clasp, with a single compartment, one open pocket and one zippered pocket, lined with charcoal gray taffeta. 13 inches by 6.5 inches by 2 inches, 1950s. *Author's collection*. $45 – 65.

Like a streamlined two-tone, late 1950s automobile, there's not much that's subtle about this handbag. Even the two-tone colors are a little edgy!

Large red straw tote, with an overlay of printed cotton in an island motif, with sailboats, surfers, and palm trees, in shades of red, green, blue, yellow, and brown, with double red straw, fabric-lined top handles, a snap closure, single compartment, one zippered pocket, and red cotton lining. 15 inches by 11 inches by 3 inches, undetermined age, very likely from the1980s. *Courtesy of Gemma Pomilio*. $25 – 45.

Large and colorful, this vintage tote, or something like it, is a must-have for summer.

Printed canvas tote, in shades of gray, red, blue, and yellow, with a vintage image of four girls waving from a convertible, with a young man driving, with additional decorative red and black glass beads, with a black vinyl bottom with brass feet, double black vinyl top handles, a zippered closure, and red nylon lining with a single compartment and one zippered pocket. 11 inches by 7 inches by 2.5 inches, undetermined age, very likely from the 1990s. *Courtesy of Gemma Pomilio*. $35 – 45.

Totes of this type always stir up a little conversation. Who wouldn't want to be in this convertible?

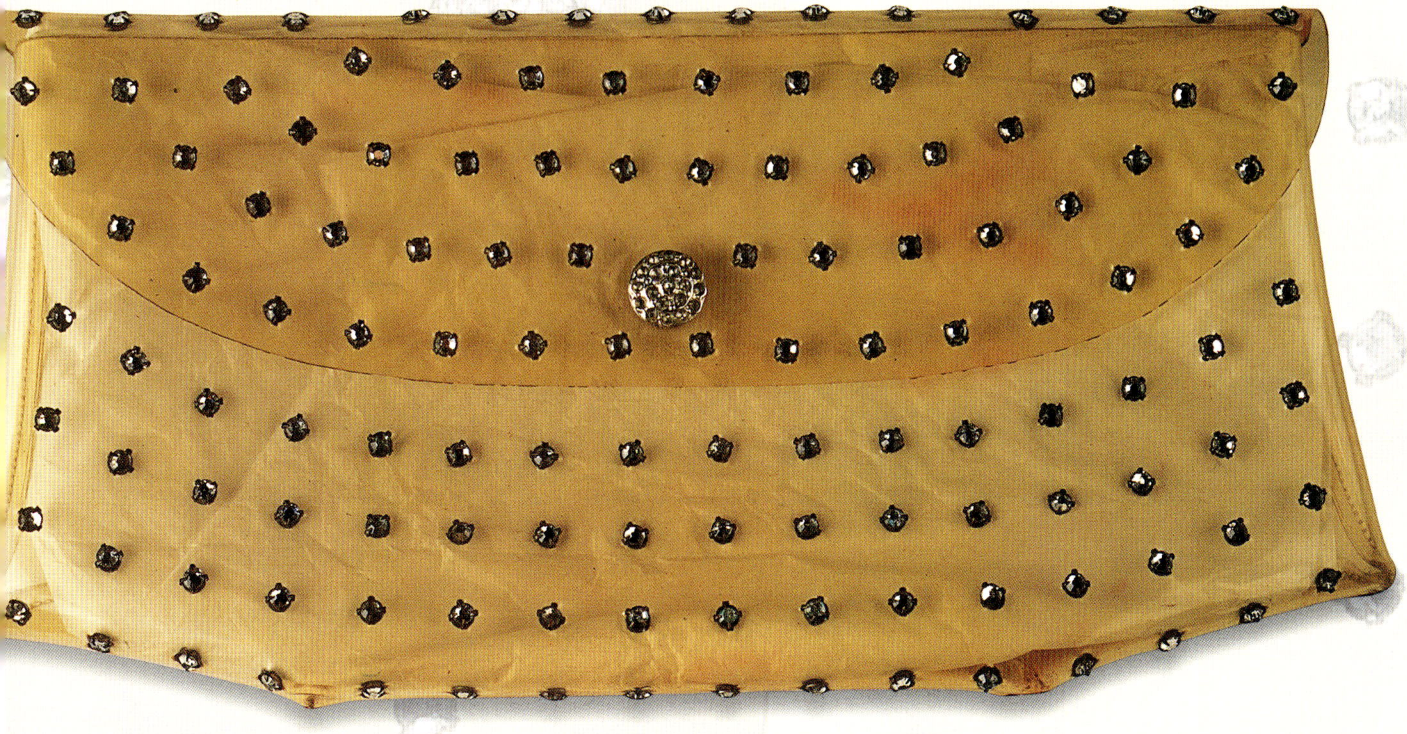

Clear plastic peek-a-boo envelope clutch, decorated with prong-set rhinestones, with a snap closure, encrusted with rhinestones. 10 inches by 5 inches by 1 inch, 1950s. *Author's collection*. $35 – 45.

This little clutch came from a time when people actually got embarrassed about some of the things they did. So, it makes me wonder how they managed with these peek-a-boo-bags.

Large black and ivory etched velour handbag, with a deep flap of black leather, a black leather top handle with a gold-tone bar decoration across the top, gold-tone, turn-lock clasp with open work, two compartments, one open pocket and one zippered pocket, and a beige leather lining. 13 inches by 11 inches by 2.5 inches, 1950s. *Author's collection, a gift from Elsie Hench*. $90 – 115.

This is a retro look you have to take seriously.

Black patent leather handbag, with gold-tone chains at each side, a double gold-tone chain handle, turn-lock clasp, with a single compartment and one open pocket, lined with black faille, gold-stamped *Lewis, Made In Italy, Genuine Patent*. 8 inches by 6 inches by 3 inches, 1960s. *Courtesy of the Family of Bernice Harris*. $75 – 95.

Take these chains away, and you'll have a much less exciting handbag.

Dark brown leather fold-over clutch, with a gold-tone handle, detailed with dark brown leather, a zippered compartment accessible from the outside, a snap closure with a single compartment, one open pocket, and a bright yellow leather lining, gold-stamped *Greta, Made In Italy*; convertible to a shoulder bag, with a gold-tone chain handle. 9.75 inches by 7.5 inches, opening to 9.75 inches by 10.75 inches, 1960s. *Courtesy of Erin Smith*. $85 – 95.

This bag can carry just enough stuff to all the fun places!

Light tan glazed straw handbag, with brass detailing and chain, and a tan vinyl lining with a gold-lined open pocket, stamped *Rodo*. 9.5 inches by 6 inches by 3 inches, 1960s. *Courtesy of the Family of Bernice Harris*. $95 – 115.

A structured straw handbag, with great detailing and élan!

Accordion bag, in a tan, green, and rose floral etched velour, trimmed with black leather, with a single black leather top handle, and two compartments, one zippered and the other open, labeled *Tano of Madrid, Made In Italy*. 9 inches by 7 inches by 3 inches, 1960s. *Courtesy of the Family of Bernice Harris*. $95 – 110.

Pouch style velour and tailored velour handbags with leather trim were very fashionable during the mid-to-late 1960s. This is a particularly good example.

Chestnut brown suede pouch style bag, with fringe at the bottom and again half way up, drawstring closure with 14-inch strap with metal ring decoration, unlined brown leather interior. 10 inches by 13 inches, 1960s. *Courtesy of Robert Browne*. $65 – 85.

Fringed bags were fashionable during the 1960s and 1970s, and this is an especially good one.

Mahogany-colored vinyl handbag, in a gathered pouch style, with grommets at each side, and a gold-tone chain handle, with a single compartment, lined with brown faille, labeled *Made In France For Saks Fifth Avenue*. 9 inches by 7 inches by 3 inches, 1960s. *Courtesy of the Family of Bernice Harris*. $65 – 85.

A charming little pouch style handbag!

Navy blue suede handbag, with a navy blue reptile-embossed vinyl strap and turn-lock closure, gold-tone chain and navy blue reptile-embossed vinyl 14-inch shoulder strap, opening to two distinct compartments, lined with navy blue faille, navy blue reptile-embossed vinyl, and tan faille, with one open pocket and one zippered pocket, gold-stamped *Block*. 7 inches by 8.5 inches by 2.5 inches, 1960s. *Author's collection*. $65 – 75.

Diverse materials and design elements are used here to create a fascinating handbag.

Orange plastic beaded handbag, with an 11.5-inch beaded top handle, zippered closure, and a single compartment with one open pocket, lined with tangerine satin, labeled *Made In Hong Kong*. 8.5 inches by 6.5 inches by 1 inch, 1960s. *Courtesy of Erin Smith.* $45 – 55.

A delightful citrus treat to complement any summer look.

Small handbag of beige raffia and beige faceted plastic beads, with a beige plastic frame and handle, flip-over ring clasp, small brass "feet," a single compartment, one zippered pocket, and a beige cotton lining, labeled *Made In Italy*. 9.5 inches by 7 inches by 4.5 inches, 1960s. *Courtesy of Erin Smith*. $65 – 75.

Beads and raffia really work well together here.

Charcoal gray embossed vinyl brief case bag, with silver-tone lock and clasp, straps with silver-tone buckles, and a single top handle. Inside, a single compartment, one zippered pocket, lined with beige vinyl. 11 inches by 8 inches by 4 inches, 1960s. *Courtesy of Erin Smith*. $45 – 65.

What gives with this vinyl embossing anyway? I must have missed seeing this one when I visited the reptile house at the zoo.

Chestnut brown patent leather handbag, with strap appliqué and gold-tone buckles, a brown patent leather covered frame, with push style gold-tone clasp, with a single compartment, one open pocket with a small makeup mirror inside, and one zippered pocket, lined with dark brown vinyl, gold-stamped *Susan Gail Original*. 7 inches by 6 inches by 4 inches, 1960s. *Courtesy of Erin Smith*. $55 – 75.

Accessorize this handbag with a pair of square-toed slingback pumps, fishnets, and a mini skirt!

Red straw accordion clutch handbag, trimmed with red patent leather, with a red patent leather shoulder strap tucked inside, a snap closure, red patent leather and red leather lining, with a single compartment and one zippered pocket, gold-stamped *Walter Katten, New York, Made In Italy*. 7.5 inches by 5.5 inches by 1.5 inches, 1960s. *Courtesy of Erin Smith*. $95 – 110.

The handbag looks exactly the same from both sides, but only one flap opens.

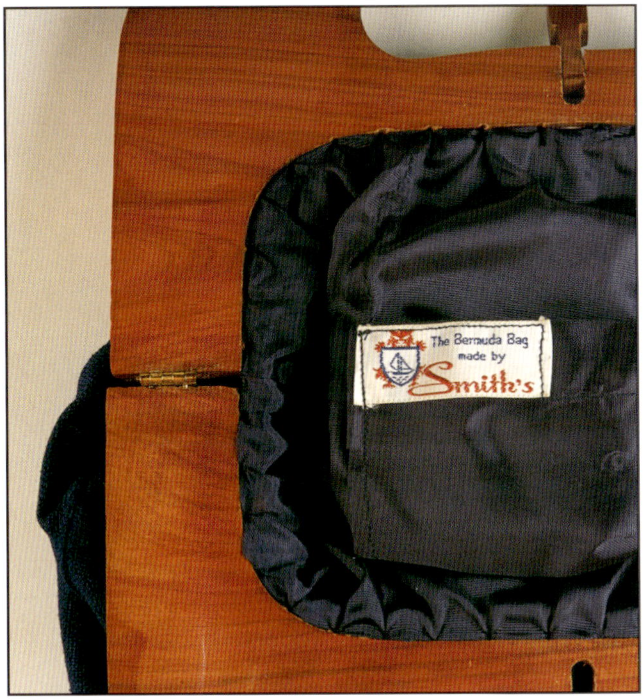

Navy blue linen, monogrammed in white cotton with the letter *P*, on a brown wooden hinged frame with integral top handle, and flip-over wooden clasp, lined with navy blue taffeta, with a single compartment and one open pocket, labeled *The Bermuda Bag, Made by Smith's*. 10.5 inches by 7 inches by 2 inches, 1960s. *Courtesy of Erin Smith*. $75 – 95.

Trendy with tourists during the late 1950s and throughout the 1960s, these classic fabric bags have become collectible in recent years.

Bright yellow glazed, reptile-embossed leather, trimmed with bone leather, with a folding chrome and gold-tone handle, as well as a narrow 15-inch bone leather shoulder strap, with a deep flap, opening to two compartments, one lined with bone leather, the other with brown leather, with two zippered pockets and one open pocket, gold-stamped *Koret, Genuine Leather*. 11 inches by 7 inches by 3 inches, 1960s. *Courtesy of Erin Smith*. $110 – 125.

How can you take a yellow handbag seriously? If it's designed and crafted by Koret, you have to take it seriously. These vintage handbags have become increasingly interesting to collectors in recent years, commanding high prices at auction.

Avocado green alligator handbag, in a rectangular shape, with a single top handle in a rounded style with gold-tone hardware, and gold-tone and faux tortoise shell plastic clasp, opening as an accordion with two distinct compartments, lined with green leather, one of which has a large, zippered pocket, unknown designer. 13 inches by 7.25 inches by 1.5 inches, 1960s. *Courtesy of Erin Smith*. $125 – 165.

At first glance, this handbag screams 1940s, but the gold-tone hardware attaching the top handle to the body of the bag is clearly 1960s, as is the plastic zipper used on the pocket inside. This bag will be out and about because it is such a great color, and it looks as good as a high-level designer handbag.

Colorful needlepoint clutch handbag, in a floral and butterfly motif, in shades of red, green, blue, orange, and lavender, on a beige ground, with a deep flap, snap closure, and light tan faille lining. 11.75 inches by 8 inches, 1960s. *Courtesy of Erin Smith*. $55 – 65.

With its bold and colorful butterflies and flowers, this clutch handbag epitomizes 1960s fashion.

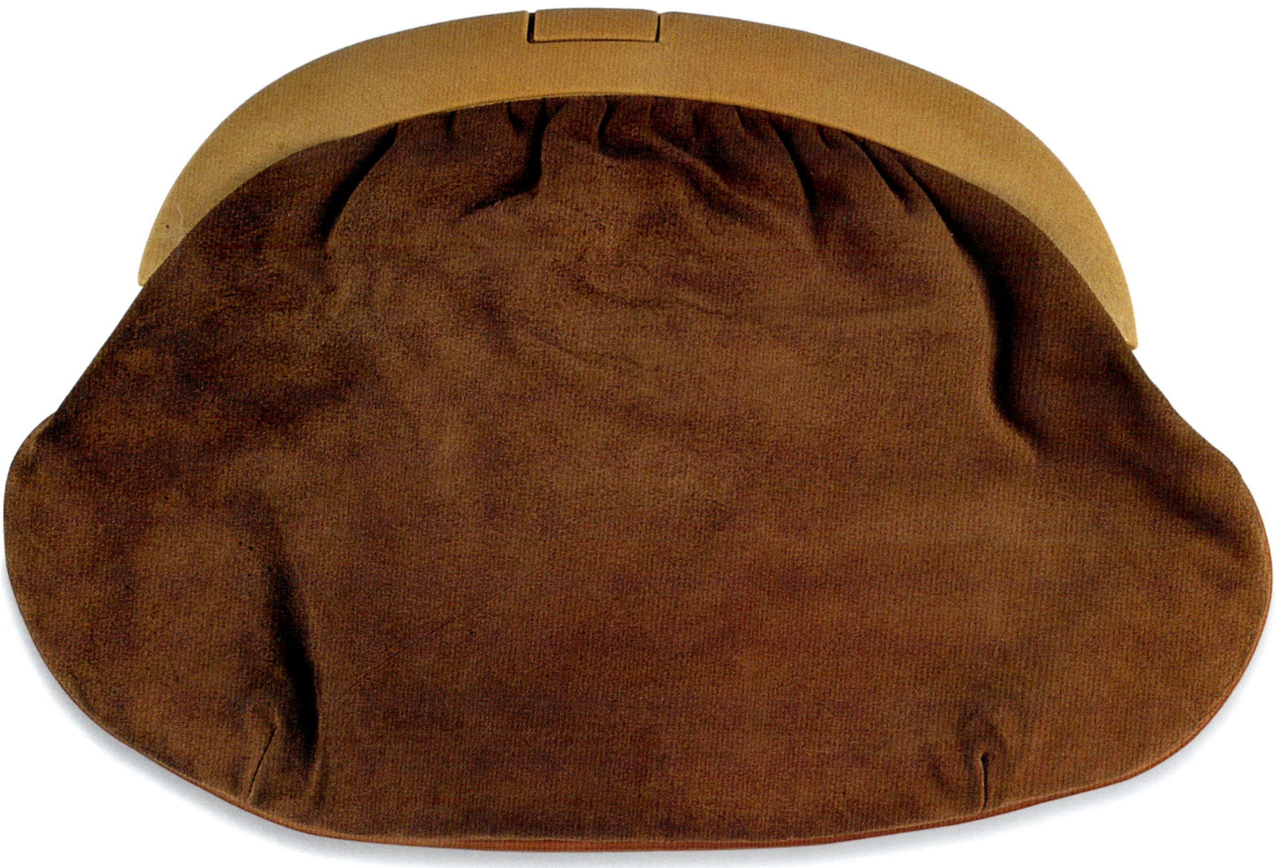

Light brown suede clutch handbag, edged in light brown leather, gathered onto a tan plastic frame with integral clasp, with a single compartment and dark brown faille lining, embossed inside frame, *Reghi, Italy*. 13 inches by 8.75 inches, 1960s. *Courtesy of Robert Browne*. $65 – 85.

Clutch handbags of this style were very popular during the early 1960s, available in leather, suede, and fabric. What makes this handbag special is its very unusual clasp, which is an integral part of its classic design.

Large velour tote, with bold orange, gold, and purple flowers with green leaves, a deep flap, 17-inch fabric handle, and single compartment lined with black taffeta. 1 inch by 12 inches by 2 inches, 1960s. *Courtesy of Erin Smith*. $45 – 65.

Popular during the 1960s, these totes have inspired some fascinating contemporary designs, especially those by H & M.

Mustard yellow leather bag, with double integral black plastic handles, snap closure just below handles, and a single compartment, lined with beige and brown monogram *RGA* linen, labeled *Roger Gimbel Accessories, Genuine Leather, Made In Hong Kong*. 10 inches by 10 inches, 1960s. *Courtesy of Erin Smith.* $65 – 85.

This handbag is unmatched for its quintessential 1960s flair!

Small black vinyl handbag, with a clasp detailed with a coral-colored plastic rose, a single black vinyl top handle, with a single compartment and one gathered pocket, lined with black faille. 8.5 inches by 6 inches by 2.5 inches, 1960s. *Courtesy of the Family of Bernice Harris. $55 – 65.*

The wonderful coral-colored plastic rose puts this handbag at the head of the pack.

Floral brocade envelope clutch, in shades of metallic gold, green, mandarin red, and mauve on a light tan ground, with a snap closure and bright red faille lining. 9 inches by 6.5 inches, 1960s. *Courtesy of Erin Smith*. $25 – 35.

A great retro chic evening purse.

Beige ostrich-embossed vinyl bag, with double Oriental-inspired brown faux tortoise plastic top handles, an outside zippered pocket, and a zippered closure, with a single compartment, lined with tan vinyl. 9.75 inches by 9.75 inches, 1960s. *Courtesy of Erin Smith*. $45 – 65.

It's hard to put a price on something like this. Can you imagine, ostrich-embossed vinyl? Of course, it shows no wear—this retro look could go on forever.

Gold-tone and Florentine gold metal oval basket bag, with a turn-lock clasp, single gold-tone top handle, single compartment lined with gold satin, and one pocket, lined with red satin, gold-stamped *Koret*, top lined with leather-embossed gold vinyl. 9 inches by 6.5 inches by 4 inches, 1960s. *Courtesy of Robert Browne*. $95 – 110.

This little gold basket is a perfect purse for evening.

Mahogany colored reptile-embossed suede bag, with a deep flap, detailed with a strap of burgundy reptile-embossed leather, held in place with two silver-tone *C* shapes; shoulder strap of mahogany colored suede, shredded into six strips, with a snap closure, single compartment, with one open pocket, and a tan faille lining, labeled *T. Elliott & Sons, London*. 11 inches by 9.5 inches by 2 inches, 1970s. *Author's collection*. $85 – 110.

The shredded strap may be unique, but seems to epitomize handbag design of the 1970s—casual, chaotic, but chic.

Brown suede handbag, trimmed with reptile-embossed brown vinyl, an H-shaped gold tone clasp with vinyl strap, a brown reptile-embossed shoulder strap, and a single compartment, one zippered pocket, and one open pocket. 11.5 inches by 7 inches by 3 inches, 1970s. *Courtesy of the Family of Bernice Harris*. $65 – 85.

The bold, H-shaped gold-tone clasp and the bold rectangular shape give this vintage handbag pizzazz.

Black quilted patent leather handbag, with a gold-tone chain and black patent leather shoulder strap, and a small gold-tone decoration on the deep flap, with a single compartment, one open pocket, lined with black faille and black patent leather. 7.5 inches by 5 inches by 2 inches, 1980s. *Courtesy of the Family of Bernice Harris*. $65 – 85.

Any high-style vintage quilted leather or quilted patent leather handbag is very fashionable. Expect to pay a big price for Chanel, of course.

Burgundy leather envelope clutch with accessories, elaborately tooled rooster motif, with additional color, leather cord edging, snap closure, and single unlined compartment, paper-labeled *Hand Made In India, 100% Leather.* 8 inches by 5 inches. Accessories include a wallet, 4 inches by 4 inches, opening to 4 inches by 8 inches, and a very small change purse, 3 inches by 2.5 inches, 1970s. *Author's collection*. $45 – 55 for the set.

Ethnic accessories always add panache.

Purple quilted reptile-embossed leather, with a deep flap, adjustable gold-tone chain and purple leather shoulder strap, which adjusts through grommets to 26 inches, labeled *Nan Duskin, Made In Canada*. 7 inches by 5 inches by 2 inches, 1980s. *Courtesy of the Family of Bernice Harris*. $65 – 85.

I believe we would all be better off if there were more purple handbags in the world.

White leather pouch style handbag, gathered under a soft white leather strap, which goes entirely around the handbag, detailed with appliqué of white snakeskin and white lizard, with a narrow 23-inch shoulder strap, and a snap-open, hinged frame, with a single compartment, one zippered pocket, and a black faille lining, designer's name is illegible. 9.5 inches by 7.5 inches by 2.5 inches, 1980s. *Author's collection*. $75 – 95.

A beautifully crafted soft leather handbag, with outstanding detailing and appliqué.

Bright red mushroom pleated satin evening bag, with gold-tone frame and fold-down gold-tone handle, trimmed with eleven prong-set rhinestones, with 22-inch gold-tone chain handle tucked inside, lined with red satin with a single compartment and one open pocket. 9 inches by 6 inches by 1.5 inches, 1980s. *Author's collection*. $25 – 35.

With an interesting texture and cheerful color, this vintage 1980s evening bag is a great alternative to some of the less inspiring contemporary evening bags in its price range.

Small cream lizard handbag, with one side made up of stripes of cream, tan, and ivory snakeskin and lizard, detailed with gold-tone *OC* insignia, with a narrow 18-inch strap, zippered closure with gold-tone *OC* pull, and light tan leather monogram lining, with *OC* and *Oleg Cassini* printed in light brown. 9.5 inches by 5 inches by 1.5 inches, 1980s. *Courtesy of Erin Smith*. $55 – 85.

True to its school, this little handbag from the 1980s does not leave us guessing about who designed it, which fits right in with the current trend.

Leather patch handbag, in plain and reptile-embossed leathers, in brown, gray, and light tan, with a brown reptile-embossed strap and gold-tone snap, as well as a zippered closure, narrow 24-inch shoulder strap, single compartment with one zippered pocket, lined with tan faille, labeled *Fifth Avenue Handbags, Made In U.S.A.* 14 inches by 10.5 inches, 1980s *Author's collection*. $45 – 65.

Patchwork handbags are either more versatile than single color handbags, or they are the forerunners of handbag clash. They have about as much harmony as a crazy patch quilt.

Colorful leather tote, with one side hot pink leather, and the other yellow leather with appliqué of colorful abstract shapes, and cord embroidery, with a narrow orange leather shoulder strap, zippered closure, black taffeta lining, with a single compartment and one zippered pocket, labeled *Samir Handbags, Made In U.S.A.* 11.5 inches by 12 inches, 1980s. *Courtesy of Gemma Pomilio*. $75 – 95.

You have to stand way back or get real close to realize that there are faces on this handbag. It's an abstract explosion of sorts, with a single flower as the only quasi-representational image. Like an abstract painting, it may not be for everyone, but it makes a statement.

Large mandarin orange clutch handbag, with decorative stitching on both sides of the clasp, three snaps, decorative vertical stitching and gathering on both sides, and a mahogany brown taffeta lining, with a single compartment and one zippered pocket. 14 inches by 9 inches, 1980s. *Courtesy of Erin Smith.* $35 – 45.

It may be a well kept secret that the leather clutch handbags from the 1980s are often available in resale and thrift shops. These clutches offer tremendous diversity of color and design.

Large leather tote, with one side entirely of white leather, and the other side of white leather, with horizontal appliqué of orange, gold, purple, green, and burgundy leather bars or stripes, with an oval bottom of green leather, 9.5 inches by 5.5 inches, zippered closure, single top handle or strap of white leather with a gold-tone chain and large ring, with a single compartment and one zippered pocket, lined with white vinyl, labeled *Genuine Leather, Made In U.S.A.* 13 inches by 10.5 inches by 3 inches, 1980s. *Author's collection*. $55 – 65.

A great summer handbag—with white anything and bare feet for a walk on the beach.

Brushed aluminum mesh bag, with silver-tone frame and 14-inch chain handle, lined with light gray silk faille, embossed on frame, *Whiting & Davis Mesh Bags, Made In U. S.A*. 7 inches by 10 inches, 1980s. *Courtesy of Erin Smith*. $75 – 95.

A classic style, reminiscent of the Whiting & Davis enameled mesh bags from the 1920s, this beautifully crafted handbag, with bolder mesh and a no-nonsense chain, can go anywhere, any time.

All That Glitters

These handbags are all about the glitter. It's that simple.

Copper satin semi-circular box style evening bag, with iridescent copper glass beading, a wide top handle with beading, snap closure, with a single compartment, one gilt-edged pocket, and a copper satin lining. 8 inches by 4 inches by 3 inches, 1940s. *Courtesy of Robert Browne*. $125 – 145.

This little brown satin evening bag looks regal.

Structural bead crochet handbag, of "blue iris," iridescent purple and dark blue glass beads, with beaded pulls and snap-open hinged frame, single beaded and knotted top handle, additionally decorated with a fringe of looped glass beads, with a single compartment, one open pocket, a matching change purse, and black satin lining. 9 inches by 8 inches by 4 inches, 1940s. *Author's collection*. $155 – 175.

I have always loved bead crochet handbags from the 1940s. In a booklet produced by the Heirloom Needlework Guild, in 1947, discussing the Melina designs for making Hiawatha Beaded Bags at home, the handbags are described variously as "Diana…lovely as a cherished myth," and "Coquette…a minx in magic beads." Additionally, the booklet acknowledges that the "regal, shimmering Hiawatha Beads" were imported from Czechoslovakia, describing the blue glass beads as a "dancing iridescence of blue iris."

Brown velvet and charcoal gray silk satin clutch handbag, embroidered in a floral and leaf design in iridescent copper glass beads, with double flaps, a snap closure, and single compartment, with one long open pocket, edged with iridescent copper glass beads, gold-stamped *Coblentz, Made In France.* 8.5 inches by 5 inches by 1.5 inches, 1950s. *Author's collection.* $65 – 85.

This small velvet clutch combines simplicity of design with a jewel-like quality.

All over rhinestone-decorated evening bag, with a gold-tone decorated clasp, chain handle, and ivory satin lining, 7 inches by 5 inches; with purse accessories, including makeup mirror, compact, cigarette lighter, and lipstick case, all decorated with rhinestones, 1950s. *Courtesy of the Family of Bernice Harris*. $225 – 250 for the set.

The 1950s was known for opulent purse accessories and jeweled dog collars.

Very unusual ivory, pink, pale blue, and gold brocade evening clutch purse, heavily embroidered with glass beads in gold, silver, white, and pink, with scrolling, diamond, and floral motifs, lifting up from its snap closures as a square, and opening to a single compartment, with one open pocket, edged with silver glass beads, lined with ivory satin, gold-stamped *Jorell Bags, Made In France*. 9.5 inches by 5.5 inches by 1.5 inches, 1950s. *Author's collection*. $175 – 225.

A very special purse, with an unusual, if not unique structure, and magnificent beading.

Iridescent purple/blue fabric clutch, trimmed with black patent leather, with a black patent leather covered frame, and a gold-tone clasp, lined with black satin, with a single compartment and one open pocket, labeled *melbourne bags*. 12.5 inches by 6 inches by 2 inches, 1960s. *Author's collection*. $45 – 55.

Unless you're going to a costume ball, you might want to pair this one with plain black patent leather pumps.

Small barrel-shaped evening pocketbook, encrusted with black glass crystals, with a snap closure, and single compartment with black silk lining, gold-stamped *Koret*. 7 inches by 4.5 inches by 2 inches, 1960s. *Courtesy of the Family of Bernice Harris*. $225 – 250.

Midnight sparkle…

Handbag and matching pumps by *Gaymode,* in metallic floral brocade, in warm shades of tangerine, tan, gold, copper, and green, trimmed with beige vinyl; pumps with pointed toes, open sides, and small button detailing; handbag with gold-tone frame and clasp, beige vinyl top handle, and a charcoal gray taffeta faille lining, with a single compartment, one zippered pocket, and a black satin label with gold script, *Gaymode.* 11 inches by 7 inches by 3 inches, late 1950s. *Author's collection*. $95 – 110 for the set.

Handbag and matching pumps by *Lois Jeans*, in gold vinyl and glitter; pumps with pointed toes, open sides with narrow straps; clutch handbag with gold-tone frame and clasp, brass chain handle ticked inside, and a black vinyl lining, with a single compartment. 9.25 inches by 2 inches, late 1950s. *Author's collection.* $65 – 85 for the set.

There's nothing like pumps with a matching handbag to give you the homogenized look fashionable during the 1950s.

Turquoise plastic beaded bag, on a base of gold metallic crochet over gold satin, with double bracelet handles, also beaded, a single compartment, lined with gold satin, with a change purse in the center, labeled *Made in Italy for Rosenfeld*. 10 inches by 5.5 inches by 3.5 inches, 1960s. *Courtesy of the Family of Bernice Harris*. $275 – 325.

What could be more striking than turquoise and gold?

Pale gray leather handbag, with rounded flap, snap closure, decorated with a half-sphere of rhinestone-encrusted clear Lucite, with double gray leather top handles, a single compartment with one open pocket, one gathered pocket, and one zippered pocket, lined with pale gray satin. 7.5 inches by 6.5 inches by 2 inches; matching gray leather pumps, with square toes, decorated with half-spheres of rhinestone-encrusted clear Lucite, and with partial heels of Lucite, also with rhinestones, gold stamped *Arc de Triomphe, les beaux sonliers de dames*, 1960s. *Author's collection*. $155 – 175 for the set.

This set epitomizes accessories fashion of the 1960s.

Iridescent copper and bronze padded leather bag, with a narrow copper leather shoulder strap, zippered closure, chocolate brown faille lining, and single compartment. 10 inches by 6 inches by 1 inch, 1980s. *Author's collection*. $35 – 45.

Believe me, no one has anything like this. How cool is that?

Chapter Five

Talks To Me

So maybe this is not for everyone. Maybe it wasn't among the vintage finds in Vogue this month. Maybe it didn't bring a bid at the last vintage auction...but it's mine.

Natural bamboo tote, with a semicircular shape, integral top handles, stamped inside, *Made In Japan*. 11 inches by 8 inches by 3 inches, 1940s. *Courtesy of Robert Browne*. $95 – 110.

This intricately crafted tote makes something of a fresh air fashion statement.

Large purple velvet clutch handbag, with puffy gathered sides, similar to a muff, a deep flap with decorative stitching, snap closure, and single compartment lined with rose-colored faille. 22 inches by 9 inches by 4 inches, 1940s. *Author's collection, purchased from Mary Efron, NYC*. $110 – 125.

While this is one of my favorites, I have to admit that it is not something you can carry everyday. When you do carry it, it's sure to be noticed.

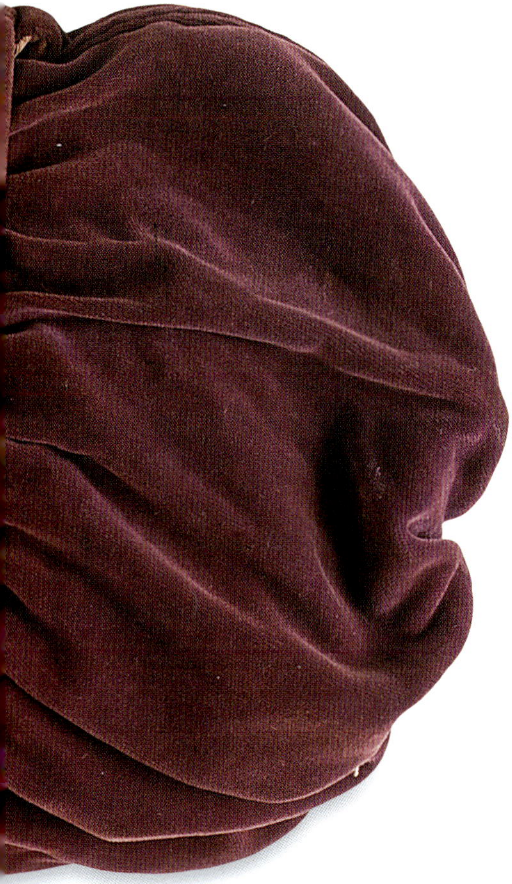

Dark brown crocheted clutch handbag, with two zippered compartments, open pockets, a wide, loop style top handle, and decorative scalloped edging and pulls. 12 inches by 7 inches, 1940s. *Courtesy of Robert Browne*. $85 – 110.

This fascinating crocheted handbag can go from day into evening with great style.

Large black flannel handbag with ornamentation, including floral needlepoint, glass beading, gold leaves, braid, and crystal, with double black flannel top handles, a gold-tone frame with gold-tone and black leather clasp, a single compartment, with one zippered pocket, and black taffeta lining, labeled *Hand Decorated Original by Caron Of Houston, Texas*. 13.25 inches by 9 inches by 2.5 inches, 1950s. *Author's collection*. $275 – 325.

Just when I thought it was safe to go back into the water, this came along! Seriously, Caron handbags are fascinating collectibles, and the term "ornamentation" almost always applies.

Unusual clear plastic-covered cotton print tote, with a Victorian carnival scene, showing a young girl on horseback, a seated lady with parasol, a gentleman wearing a skimmer style hat, another gentleman with balloons, further detailed with rhinestones, glass beads, and sequins, in shades of pink, black, gray, and red, on a gray and white striped ground, lined with beige faille, with a single compartment, one zippered and two open pockets, and a small matching change purse, attached with a fine gold chain, gold-stamped label is illegible. 12.5 inches by 11 inches by 3 inches, 1950s. *Courtesy of Gemma Pomilio*. $325 – 375.

This handbag is for the fashion courageous. In other words, you have to have a unique style of dressing to carry this one off successfully! It probably belongs behind glass.

Tan straw tote, with a net of tan braided raffia with integral handles, detailed with colorful wooden beads, with a single compartment with one zippered pocket, and a beige vinyl lining. 10.5 inches by 5.5 inches by 6 inches, labeled *Hand Made In Japan*, 1950s. *Courtesy of Gemma Pomilio*. $125 – 150.

The unique and creative combination of materials makes this an outstanding summer handbag.

Pale tangerine satin handbag, designed in a basketweave pattern under clear plastic, with a pale tangerine satin frame and clasp, also covered in clear plastic, and a heavy gold-tone chain handle, with a single compartment, one open pocket with gilt edging, and one zippered pocket, lined with pale tangerine satin, gold stamped *Created by International.* 10 inches by 13 inches, 1950s. *Author's collection.* $175 – 225.

Tan straw and raffia basket bag, with a single brown leather top handle, brown leather strap with decorated gold-tone hardware and turn-lock clasp, a single compartment and leather patch inside top, gold-stamped *Made Expressly For Jana, Made In Hong Kong*. 11 inches by 5.5 inches by 5 inches, 1960s. *Courtesy of Erin Smith*. $75 – 95.

This small vintage oval-shaped basket bag is huge on style!

Tan and white pony fur briefcase bag, trimmed with tan leather, with double tan leather top handles, a single compartment with one zippered pocket, lined with brown faille. 13 inches by 10 inches by 3 inches, 1960s. *Courtesy of the Family of Bernice Harris*. $175 – 225.

Pony fur handbags continue to be fascinating to specialized collectors.

Two velvet pouch style, fold-over clutch handbags, one warm dark brown, the other black, both with grapes and leaves appliqué in a trapunto effect, in shades of blue, green, purple, and burgundy, lined with beige taffeta faille, stamped *by Helene*. 9 inches by 6.5 inches, opening to 9 inches by 13 inches, 1960s. *Courtesy of the Family of Bernice Harris*. $150 – 175 each.

These clutch handbags have a lot of charm, and are great accents with any fashion look.

Tote in a cotton paisley print, in shades of green, gold, red, and black, with double rounded top handles, opening to a burgundy rayon lining, with two compartments and a zippered pocket in the center, labeled *Margaret Smith, Gardiner, Maine*. 13 inches by 10.5 inches by 4 inches, 1960s. *Courtesy of Gemma Pomilio*. $85 – 125.

Who would have guessed that the Margaret Smith handbags would become hot collectibles? The lesson here is that the styles are timeless, fabrics diverse and interesting, and craftsmanship excellent.

Large black leather tote or briefcase bag, with a single black leather top handle, gold-tone hardware and clasp, and small rectangular gold-tone metal embossed figural decoration, lined with pale gray leather, with a single compartment, one zippered and one open pocket. 13 inches by 11.5 inches by 2 inches, very likely made in Italy, 1960s. *Author's collection*. $125 – 175.

This is a large and beautifully crafted handbag. What makes it fascinating is the figural decoration, but it's impossible to discern what exactly these little figures are doing.

Plastic clutch purse, in the shape of a folded magazine, with paper magazine cover for "Elegance, Paris," brown faux leather strap with silver-tone buckle over snap closure, with a single compartment and one open pocket, lined with black taffeta. 12 inches by 6 inches by 2 inches, 1970s. *Courtesy of Erin Smith*. $75 – 110.

The actual clutch is made of white plastic, and the "magazine cover" used was printed to show the edges of the pages, as if the magazine were actually folded or rolled up. A fascinating, fun concept for a clutch purse!

Red fox fur and black leather handbag, with a black leather top handle, and additional 18-inch chain handle, opening to a black faille interior, with two zippered compartments, gold-stamped *Greta.* 11 inches by 11 inches by 4 inches, 1970s. *Courtesy of the Family of Bernice Harris*. $275 – 325.

What do you wear with an accessory that looks like this? Black, of course!

Two little barrel bags, one in light burgundy suede with gold-tone ends, detailing, and clasp, with a 15-inch burgundy suede strap, single compartment, lined with black leather, labeled *Made in Italy*. 9 inches by 5 inches by 3 inches; identical bag in green suede, 1970s. *Courtesy of the Family of Bernice Harris*. $125 – 145 each.

Italian handbags have always gained applause, for fine craftsmanship and materials. These two little barrel bags are no exception.

Black leather pouch style handbag, with black leather fringe on one side, with a silver-tone and embossed black leather *Harley Davidson Motor Cycles* insignia, 18-inch black leather strap, zippered closure with a single compartment, and one zippered pocket, lined with black cotton, labeled *Licensed By Harley Davidson, Made In U.S.A.* 13.5 inches by 10.5 inches; undetermined age, very likely from the 1980s. *Courtesy of Robert Browne*. $175 – 225.

This handbag definitely goes to the Harley Davidson slogan: "Define Your World In A Whole New Way."

Small gray plastic bag, with a 20-inch gold-tone chain handle, gold-tone clasp with small chain and gold-tone drop, and a single compartment, lined with tan ultra suede, labeled *Made In Italy Expressly For Rappi*. 8.5 inches by 3 inches by 5 inches, 1980s. *Courtesy of the Family of Bernice Harris*. $225 – 275.

You can't help but give this little handbag a second glance. Perhaps a melon inspired it.

Large floral printed quilted cotton tote, in shades of white and green on a black ground, with double 15 inch matching fabric top handles, an outside patch pocket with Velcro closing, zippered closure, and single compartment, with two open pockets, and black and white plaid print cotton lining , as well as partial floral print lining, labeled *Vera Bradley*. 15-inches by 13 inches by 3.5 inches, 1990s. *Courtesy of Judy Murray.* $55 – 75.

Handbags by Vera Bradley have one major distinction—they are washable. Reminiscent of knitting bags from the 1940s, they are designed with soft shapes of 100% cotton floral prints. The company was started in Fort Wayne, Indiana, in March 1982, by Barbara Bradley and Patricia Miller, to provide excellent quality, stylish quilted cotton luggage. It expanded to include handbags and accessories in various styles and designs, with names like "Bitsey" and "Bitty Betsy," in fabrics such as "Nantucket Red" and "Sherbet." Styles and patterns are periodically "retired."

Rectangular soft box bag in quilted cotton, in shades of pink and rose on a royal blue ground, with double 15-inch matching fabric top handles, a zippered closure, with one compartment, one zippered pocket, and red and white polka dot lining, as well as partial floral print lining, labeled *Vera Bradley*. 12 inches by 6.5 inches by 6 inches approximately, 1990s. *Courtesy of Judy A. Moyer.* $45 – 65.

Reminiscent of the floral printed cotton handbags designed by Margaret Smith, as well as the contemporary designs of Kate Spade, Vera Bradley handbags are bound to become serious collectibles in the future.

Chapter Six

Rodeo Drive

These handbags are for heavy duty, serious shoppers only. All others step aside.

Black acrylic oval box bag with a molded black acrylic top handle, a brass clasp detailed with black acrylic, a mirror inside the top, labeled *Wilardy.* 7.25 inches by 4.5 inches by 5.25 inches, 1950s. *Courtesy of Robert Browne*. $450 – 475.

Wilardy Originals were manufactured in the New York area during the 1950s. Known for fine craftsmanship and solid colors, these handbags, in excellent condition, are highly prized by collectors. On the lighter side, black goes with everything, and with a black Wilardy you can catch a glimpse of how you look, how your date looks, and how the people at the next table look.

Tiny velvet box style handbag, in a geometric signature print in shades of pink, purple, green, orange, black, white, dark blue, and tan, with gold-tone turn-lock clasp and a single gold-tone top handle, with a single compartment and one open pocket, lined with bright orange leather, gold-stamped *Emilio Pucci*. 5 inches by 6 inches by 3.75 inches, 1960s. *Courtesy of the Family of Bernice Harris*. $550 – 750.

It's not about the design of the handbag—it's all about the design of the fabric.

Black leather pouch style bag with gilt paint, detailed with diminutive gold and black rhinestones, with a Florentine gold frame, also detailed with gold and black rhinestones, 20-inch gold-tone chain handle, single compartment with one open pocket, lined with black silk, gold-tone labeled *Judith Leiber*. 7 inches by 7 inches by 2.5 inches, 1970s. *Courtesy of the Family of Bernice Harris*. $650 – 950.

Reminiscent of a little girl's pocketbook…but oh, so sophisticated!

Brown leather handbag, with an elaborate gold-tone frame, two small gold-tone *Rs,* attached with nuts or studs, two brown leather top handles, with a single compartment, one open pocket and one zippered pocket, lined with brown leather, gold-stamped *By Roberta Di Camerino, Product of Italy*. 11 inches by 6 inches by 4.5 inches, 1970s. *Courtesy of the Family of Bernice Harris*. $475 – 550.

Handbags by Roberta Di Camerino have become increasingly desirable in recent years, commanding high prices at auction.

Soft red woven leather bag, with double heavy gold-tone chain handles, with a single compartment, one zippered pocket, lined with tan leather, gold-tone labeled *Bottega Veneta, Made In Italy*. 10 inches by 8.5 inches by 3 inches, 1980s. *Courtesy of the Family of Bernice Harris*. $550 – 750.

A beautifully crafted handbag in a truly dramatic color!

Navy blue and gray monogram canvas tote, trimmed with navy blue leather, with gold-tone *Gucci* insignia, double navy blue leather top handles, labeled *Made In Italy By Gucci*. 17 inches by 18 inches, 1980s. *Courtesy of the Family of Bernice Harris*. $375 – 425.

According to John Peacock, Gucci was founded as a saddle shop in Florence, Italy in 1906 by Guccio Gucci. The shortage of leather during the Second World War led to the introduction of its signature canvas, with red and green striped panel and double-G Gucci motif.

Black monogram canvas satchel, trimmed with black leather, with double black leather top handles, gold-tone hardware, red and green vertical stripes, a zippered closure, a single compartment, lined with black canvas, labeled *Made In Italy By Gucci*. 14 inches by 9 inches by 8.5 inches, 1980s. *Courtesy of the Family of Bernice Harris*. $375 – 425.

The subtle black monogram canvas makes this satchel especially attractive and versatile.

Brown and tan monogram canvas, with open work and a large gold-tone double-*G* insignia on its deep flap, brown pigskin trim and single top handle, with a single compartment and one zippered pocket, lined with tan suede, labeled *Gucci of Italy*. 12 inches by 9.5 inches by 1.5 inches, 1980s. *Courtesy of the Family of Bernice Harris*. $425 – 475.

A fascinating use of the double-G gold-tone insignia, combined with the monogram canvas.

Quilted black leather box style bag, with single black leather top handle, with a gold-tone chain and black leather shoulder strap, black leather clasp with gold-tone double-*C* insignia, a single compartment, one zippered pocket and one open pocket, lined with black leather, gold-stamped *Chanel.* 7.5 inches by 5.5 inches by 3 inches, 1980s, with original box. *Courtesy of the Family of Bernice Harris*. $850 – 1200.

To quote directly from Fairchild's Dictionary of Fashion, by the 1960s "her (Chanel's) trademarks were the Chanel suit—braid-trimmed, collarless jacket, patch pockets, and knee-length skirt in soft Scottish tweeds; multiple gold chain necklaces with fake jewels; chain-handled quilted handbags; beige and black slingback pumps; flat black hair bows, and a gardenia."

White quilted leather box style bag, with white leather clasp with gold-tone double-*C* insignia, 19-inch gold-tone chain and white leather shoulder strap, with a single compartment, one zippered pocket, and one open pocket, lined with white leather, gold-stamped *Chane*l. 7 inches by 6 inches by 2.5 inches, 1980s. *Courtesy of the Family of Bernice Harris*. $850 – 1200.

A classic style that never grows old!

Chapter Seven

Classic Vintage

These handbags are pure vintage. They can either make you look very old, or they can give you that cutting-edge style that you crave. Be careful!

Dark brown suede clutch handbag, with four decorative brass studs or nuts, opening to two separate compartments of dark brown leather and dark brown suede, with a brass bar in the center, each compartment lined with brown silk. 9 inches by 5.5 inches, opening to 9 inches by 11 inches, 1930s. *Courtesy of Robert Browne*. $110 – 125.

Structurally interesting would be an understatement here. This is the most unusual clutch handbag I have seen.

Black leather clutch purse, with sculptural detailing on one side, and an attached strap on the other side, silver-tone metal frame and clasp with an elaborate embossed drop, decorated with marcasites, a single compartment with one open pocket, black taffeta lining, and change purse with silver-tone metal frame attached at center. 9.5 inches by 5.25 inches by 1.5 inches, 1930s. *Courtesy of Robert Browne*. $95 – 110.

This small clutch is sculptural and fascinating.

Large brown alligator handbag, with a 15-inch, heavy brass chain handle, two compartments and two open pockets, with attached purse with frame in the center, gold-stamped *Koret, Made of Alligator*. 10.5 inches by 9.5 inches by 3.5 inches, 1940s. *Courtesy of Robert Browne*. $450 – 525.

Koret handbags have recently found their place at auction, commanding increasingly high prices. I am reminded of a little pamphlet I found in a vintage Koret I once owned, describing how Dick Koret designed various inside pockets for all his handbags, "to hold your compact, lipstick, comb, cigarette case or other out-sized impedimenta." I like the concept of "impedimenta" when it comes to the contents of a handbag.

Brown alligator is as classic vintage as it gets and don't forget the jump rope rhyme, "The Lady With the Alligator Purse," which goes something like this: "Miss Lucy had a baby, His name was Tiny Tim, She put him in the bathtub, To see if he could swim. He drank up all the water, He ate up all the soap, He tried to eat the bathtub, but it wouldn't go down his throat. Miss Lucy called the doctor, Miss Lucy called the nurse, and Miss Lucy called the lady, with the alligator purse."

Mustard yellow lizard box bag, with gold-tone frame and clasp, single mustard yellow lizard top handle, lined with black faille, single compartment, with one open pocket, an attached black faille change purse, and a black faille lining. 8.5 inches by 5 inches by 4 inches, 1940s. *Courtesy of Erin Smith*. $125 – 145.

Although classic vintage, this lizard handbag is a most unusual color.

Navy blue velvet pouch style bag, with an unusual horseshoe-shaped brass clasp with rounded navy blue velvet handle, single compartment with one open pocket and a navy blue satin lining, labeled *Garay*. 8.5 inches by 7.5 inches by 2 inches, 1940s. *Courtesy of Robert Browne*. $110 – 125.

The way the clasp slips over the rounded velvet handle is really fascinating—and most unusual.

Very small dark brown leather handbag, with a dark brown leather-covered frame, clear Lucite cube clasp, and double dark brown leather top handles, with a single compartment, one open pocket, and a brown taffeta lining. 7.5 inches by 6 inches by 3.25 inches, 1940s. *Courtesy of Erin Smith*. $55 – 75.

This classic little handbag can go anywhere. Sorry…but it is cute!

Ivory nylon crinkle crepe pouch style bag, gathered onto a white plastic frame, with clasp, and double fabric top handles. 8 inches by 7.5 inches by 3.5 inches, 1940s. *Courtesy of Robert Browne*. $55 – 75.

A delightful little handbag—and unusual in crinkle crepe.

Light brown crocheted clutch handbag, with a zippered closure, decorated with a crocheted pull, with a single compartment, one open pocket, and a brown taffeta lining with matching change purse. 13.5 inches by 7.5 inches, 1940s. *Courtesy of Robert Browne*. $75 – 95.

Although classic vintage, this warm brown crocheted clutch looks great with contemporary fashion.

Black suede handbag, with a black grosgrain ribbon top handle, gold-tone frame and clasp, and gold-tone initials, *FRT* on front of handbag, which has some decorative tailoring and gathering, with a single compartment, one open pocket, and a black taffeta lining. 9.75 inches by 6.5 inches by 2 inches, 1940s. *Courtesy of Robert Browne*. $65 – 85.

The point about vintage handbags is that they once belonged to someone else, and seeing someone else's initials placed boldly on the front of the handbag confirms that. It's kind of comforting to know that this handbag was picked at least twice!

Brown cordé handbag, with a brass frame and clasp, single brown cordé top handle, with a single compartment, two open pockets, one zippered pocket, gold chain with small pencil attached, and chestnut brown satin lining. 8.25 inches by 7.5 inches, 1940s. *Courtesy of Robert Browne*. $110 – 125.

Cordé handbags have always been the show with vintage collectors. This one is a particularly nice example of triangular shapes within a slightly modified square.

Small navy blue cordé handbag, with a zippered closure, loop style handle, a single compartment, one open pocket, and a navy blue taffeta lining, labeled *Styled By Normandie*. 8.5 inches by 6 inches, 1940s. *Courtesy of Robert Browne*. $95 – 110.

Cordé handbags were actually composed of rows of gimp, or heavy core yarn, stitched to a background fabric to make a pattern.

Cream enameled links or mesh, with a bold ivory Bakelite frame with a bamboo look, ivory Bakelite chain type top handle, navy blue faille lining, with a single compartment and one open pocket, labeled *Alumesh, Whiting & Davis Co. Mesh Bags, Made In U.S.A*. 10.5 inches by 6.5 inches by 2 inches, 1940s. *Author's collection*. $175 – 225.

This handbag is probably older than Grandma, but it has serious vintage appeal.

Black flannel handbag, in an unusual triangular shape, with a floral gilt-decorated frame with clasp, decorated with small colorful rhinestones, a black flannel top handle, a single compartment with two open pockets, lined with black satin, labeled *Charlet Bag, Paris, New York*. 9 inches by 8 inches by 3 inches, 1940s. *Courtesy of Robert Browne*. $185 – 225.

This fabric handbag, with its exceptional structure and decoration, raises the bar for classic vintage.

Tan alligator handbag, with baby alligator appliqué; body of alligator partially on top of handbag with head slightly down first flap, main body and tail of alligator on the other side of the handbag, with two flaps and snap closures, brown leather edging, adjustable single top handle with snaps, with a single compartment lined with tan flannel, similar to contemporary moleskin, stamped with a small alligator, *Made In Cuba*. 8.5 inches by 6 inches by 3 inches, 1950s. *Courtesy of Robert Browne.* $350 – 450.

It was not uncommon to see these tan alligator handbags for sale in souvenir shops in Florida during the 1950s. What makes this one special is the very unusual placement of the baby alligator. It is also unusual to find one of these handbags in excellent condition, as too often the adjustable handles became dry and brittle, and cracked and fell off.

Butterscotch colored molded plastic oval box bag, with subtle red lines in the plastic, a molded plastic handle, plastic "S" clasp with brass fittings, and a small faceted gold-tone decoration at the center of the top or lid. 7.5 inches by 4.5 inches by 4 inches, 1950s. *Courtesy of Robert Browne*. $225 – 250.

A great little box bag with warmth and charm.

Taupe, cowhide-embossed vinyl handbag, with a bold rectangular shape and integral handle, with gold-tone frame and clasp, opening to a single compartment with one zippered pocket, lined with beige vinyl. 15 inches by 8.5 inches by 1.5 inches, 1960s. *Author's collection*. $45 – 65.

Vinyl handbags were much less expensive than leather handbags. In the vintage marketplace they have become very desirable collectibles. Generally they show almost no wear—but then we expected to hear that, didn't we?

Special occasion handbag of white satin, embroidered on both sides with round, white glass beads and iridescent white/mauve sequins, with a gold-tone, five-sided filigreed handle, and a gold-tone frame and clasp, with a filigreed drop, lined with peach-colored satin, with one compartment and a single open pocket, labeled *Bag By Debbie, Made In Hong Kong*. 9 inches by 6.5 inches, 1960s. *Author's collection*. $95 – 105.

This is the quintessential wedding guest's handbag. Rules of etiquette aside, put this delicious handbag right on the table where it belongs!

Diminutive floral printed silk handbag, in rich shades of red, purple, yellow, blue, fuchsia, gold, and tan, with an unusual matching rolled silk top handle, flap and snap closure, and beige faille lining, with a single compartment and three open pockets, one of which has a scalloped edge, and floral printed silk lining, another holds a small, unused makeup mirror. 7 inches by 5.5 inches by 1.5 inches, 1960s. *Author's collection*. $75 – 95.

You'll want to have this floral printed silk handbag hanging ever so daintily from your wrist, as you sip your Long Island iced tea at the garden party. Who knows where your white gloves are? Who cares anyway? Maybe the waiter carried them away with the last tray of drinks.

Paisley brocade handbag, in shades of gold metallic, bright green, orange, and blue on a black ground, with a gold mesh top handle, two side pockets lined with ivory satin, a gold-tone clasp, single compartment with two open pockets, also lined with ivory satin, gold-stamped *andrew geller*. 9 inches by 6 inches by 3 inches, 1960s. *Courtesy of the Family of Bernice Harris*. $150 – 175.

Andrew Geller shoes and handbags are classic styles and beautifully crafted.

Black glazed leather handbag, with an elaborate gold-tone emblem of a lion and horse on the deep flap, with a single black leather adjustable top handle, with a single compartment with change purse, gold-stamped *Koret*. 9 inches by 7 inches by 3.5 inches, 1960s. *Courtesy of the Family of Bernice Harris*. $175 – 225.

The gold-tone emblem takes this traditional handbag to a different place.

Black patent leather handbag, trimmed with ivory colored vinyl, with a decorative clasp, detailed with a cylindrical piece of ivory colored vinyl, gold-tone and black patent leather chain, with a single compartment, one zippered pocket, and one open pocket, lined with black faille, gold-stamped *Stylecraft.* 8 inches by 6 inches by 3.5 inches, 1960s. *Courtesy of the Family of Bernice Harris*. $95 – 110.

Its unusual clasp and ivory vinyl detailing make this handbag a very good vintage choice.

Chapter Eight

Wish List

I just wish I owned these handbags. That's all.

Ivory enameled mesh handbag, with an enameled mesh fringe, Florentine finished brass frame and clasp, with a 14-inch chain handle, lined with peach colored silk faille, with a single compartment, stamped inside frame and with label, *Whiting & Davis Co. Mesh Bags, Made In U. S. A.* 5.5 inches by 8.5 inches, with fringe, 1940s. *Courtesy of George Wilmot.* $85 – 110.

This is one versatile little evening bag. In fact, it's so versatile it could be carried during the day, without looking over-the-top.

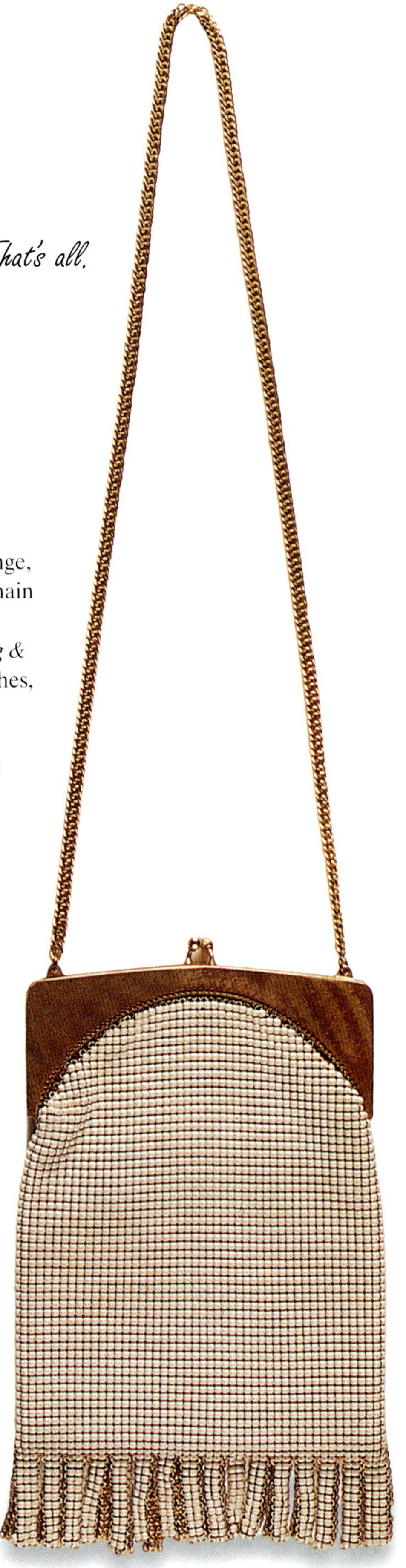

Brown suede tailored handbag, with identical sides, both with vertical brown suede stripe appliqué, single brown suede top handle, brown suede-covered, hinged snap-open frame, with a single compartment with two open pockets, one containing a change purse which matches the chestnut brown satin lining. 9 inches by 8.25 inches by 3.5 inches, 1940s. *Courtesy of Robert Browne*. $150 – 175.

The most structurally perfect handbag I have seen, this one is close to the top of the wish list!

Marbleized Lucite handbag, with flecks of gold and silver embedded in the molded Lucite body, with clear Lucite top and sides, etched with a floral design, and double molded plastic top handles, also with flecks, as well as a molded plastic clasp, brass fittings and hinges, and small clear plastic semi-circular feet, labeled *Patricia of Miami.* 7.5 inches by 6 inches by 2.5 inches, 1950s. *Courtesy of Robert Browne*. $375 – 425.

Morty Edelstein, who was the manufacturer of Miami Handbags, and the "Mor" of Fre-Mor bags, added the Patricia of Miami line, named for his wife, Patricia Edelstein. If you ask me, this is a lot better than having a boat named after you, and these bags are fabulous!

Black velvet, box-style handbag, with a black velvet "jewel-decorated" clasp, single black braided velvet top handle, and a single compartment with one open pocket, lined with red satin, gold-stamped *Ingber, Made In U.S.A*. 8 inches by 4.5 inches by 4 inches, 1950s. *Courtesy of Erin Smith*. $155 – 175.

Ingber is known for creative design, and excellent craftsmanship.

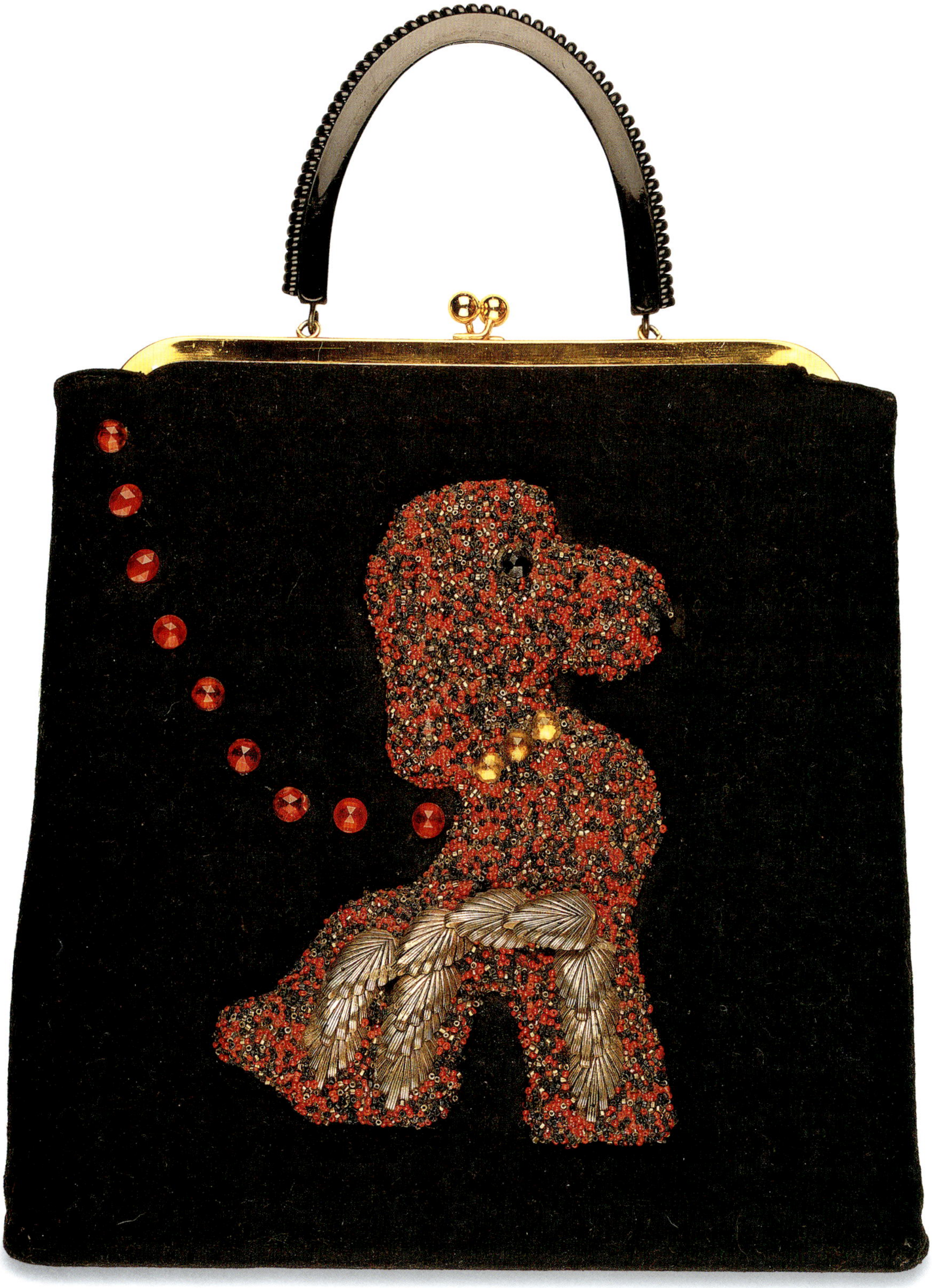

Black wool fabric handbag, with a gold-tone frame and clasp, black molded plastic handle, poodle dog appliqué in red, gold, and black glass beads, with a leash of red faceted crystal, collar of gold faceted crystal, eye and nose of black faceted crystal, additionally decorated with twelve brass paillettes or spangles, lined with black taffeta, with a single compartment and two open pockets. 11.5 inches by 11 inches by 3 inches, 1950s. *Courtesy of Robert Browne*. $375 – 425.

This poodle is Best of Show!

Unusual round red leather handbag, with circular red leather appliqué, a small gold-tone circle near the top, zippered closure and 28-inch, red leather shoulder strap, with gold-tone buckle, lined with red cotton/rayon damask, with a single compartment, and one zippered pocket, gold-tone labeled *Movado, Made In Italy*. 9 inches in diameter, late 1980s. *Courtesy of Linda J. Munson*. $550 – 625.

Reminiscent of the face of a Movado watch, this handbag will turn heads, not because it's gimmicky, but because it raises the bar on elegance.

Chapter Nine

Pure Gold

Pure gold is only ostensibly an accessory. Pure gold is so serious that it should be worn with a full-length mink coat, or with the most exquisite evening gown you can afford. It is so serious; maybe it shouldn't even be worn...

Red silk velvet evening bag with ruching, a fabric handle attached with small brass rings, a zippered closure, and gold silk satin lining, with a single compartment, one open pocket, a matching change purse, and a small mirror, edged with gold silk, gold-stamped *Graceline*. 8.5 inches by 5.5 inches by 2.5 inches, 1940s. *Author's collection*. $150 – 175.

This little red velvet gem is small and luxurious, with a hint of decadence.

Black satin evening bag, with a brass frame, hinged to open fully in a modified heart shape, a single knotted black satin top handle, and a black satin lining. 5.5 inches by 6.5 inches by 2 inches, 1940s. *Courtesy of Robert Browne*. $175 – 225.

An exquisite evening bag!

Black wool pouch style handbag, with ruching, a drawstring closure and clear Lucite detailing, with a single compartment, one open pocket, and a black satin lining. 11.5 inches by 8 inches by 7 inches, 1940s. *Courtesy of Robert Browne*. $165 – 185.

This handbag defies further analysis—it's just very unusual. The world is a better place with it around—that's all!

Black faille pouch style handbag, with engraved gold-tone compact top or lid, with unused compact with mirror, single black faille knotted top handle, with a single compartment, lined with black taffeta, and a black taffeta change purse, labeled *Comus 1947*. 5.5 inches by 5.5 inches by 4.5 inches. *Courtesy of Robert Browne*. $225 – 250.

An exquisite little handbag and a jewel of a compact—all in one!

Clutch style handbag, made of aluminum mesh, of hundreds of small round disks, each perforated with four small holes and linked to adjoining disks, with a back strap and zippered closure with ring pull. 9 inches by 7 inches, with a matching 2-inch wide belt, 1940s. *Author's collection*. $375 – 425 for the set.

For one thing, it's very unusual to find a handbag with a matching belt from the 1940s (or for that matter from any decade). To find large-scale aluminum mesh, without enamel, is also rare. Let's just face it; this might be the most unusual set I have come across.

Drum box style handbag, elaborately embellished on one side with floral printed velvet, needlepoint flowers, glass beading, gold rickrack, and colorful faceted crystal; the other side of black fabric, trimmed with gold rickrack, the frame of pierced chrome, with a single black fabric top handle, two black taffeta-lined compartments. 7 inches in diameter with four ball "feet," labeled *Hand Decorated by Caron of Houston, Texas*, 1940s. *Author's collection*. $150 – 175.

"Rosie the Riveter" would have loved this handbag!

HAND DECORATED ORIGINAL
by
Caron
OF HOUSTON, TEXAS

Blush pink leather tailored handbag, with a sculptural flap, with a gold-tone "shield" shaped decoration, single blush pink leather top handle, single compartment with one open pocket with a small makeup mirror inside, and one zippered pocket, lined with black satin, gold-stamped *Lencraft By Lennox*. 7.5 inches by 9.5 inches by 1.25 inches, 1950s. *Author's collection, purchased from The Bag Lady,* $150 – 165.

One of the most sculptural handbags I have seen, this handbag is almost paper thin.

Small reptile-embossed gold leather handbag, with a gold-tone frame and clasp, double top handles, and a single compartment with one open pocket, lined with peach colored satin, labeled *HL, U.S.A*. 7 inches by 5.5 inches by 3.25 inches, 1960s. *Courtesy of Erin Smith*. $65 – 85.

Have you ever seen a gold alligator? I think not.

Tiny gold plated evening purse, monogrammed *GG*, designed to look traditional, with a 22-inch chain, and black velvet lining, gold-stamped *Gucci A Collection, Made In Italy*. 4 inches by 3.5 inches by 2 inches, 1970s. *Courtesy of George Wilmot.* $550 – 650.

Like an Olympic Gold Medal, this purse is the show! Diminutive, with a childlike simplicity, it is pure luxury.

Gold molded plastic oval box bag, with an etched Lucite top with starburst and leaf pattern, molded Lucite top handle with decoration, chrome clasp, labeled *Saks Fifth Avenue*. 7.5 inches by 5 inches by 4.5 inches, 1950s. *Courtesy of Robert Browne*. $325 – 375.

The only accessory this handbag needs is a strapless black cocktail dress.

Metallic silver and white brocade evening bag, detailed above the integral handle with a silver kidskin tie, flap with snap closure, opening to a single compartment, lined with ivory silk satin, with two open pockets, lined with gold satin, one of which contains a small pouch with make-up mirror, one zippered compartment, and a small change purse attached with a fine gold chain, gold stamped *Koret Tresor*, with insignia. 9.5 inches by 10 inches, early 1960s. *Author's collection*. $175 – 225.

One of my favorites, and a fine example of Koret craftsmanship, this handbag has great charm.

Soft gold kidskin pouch style evening purse, gathered onto a gold kidskin-covered frame, with a gold-tone clasp with two large spheres, encrusted with rhinestones, double chain handles, a single compartment, lined with peach colored satin, and two open pockets, one with a small peach colored satin pouch. 7.5 inches by 5.5 inches by 2 inches, 1960s. *Courtesy of Erin Smith.* $150 – 175.

In flawless condition, this evening handbag gives new meaning to the Midas touch.

Gold tone minaudiere in the shape of a small sleeping kitten, with a ribbon collar of gold, red, and green crystals, a gold leather base and lining, with accessories, including a gold-tone change purse, mirror, and comb, labeled *Judith Leiber*. 7 inches by 3 inches by 4 inches, 1970s. *Courtesy of the Family of Bernice Harris*. $850 – 1500.

A cunning little handbag! John Peacock, in his book Fashion Accessories, The Complete 20th Century Sourcebook, credits Leiber with "artistry and technique" and calls her "endlessly inventive."

Small, pear-shaped, gold-tone purse with Florentine finish and crystal decoration in a petal effect, with a gold-tone clasp, and 15-inch gold-tone chain handle, with a single compartment, lined with gold kidskin, silver-stamped *Judith Leiber*. 5.5 inches by 6 inches by 2 inches, 1970s. *Courtesy of the Family of Bernice Harris*. $750 – 1200.

Truly a jewel!

1939 New York World's Fair evening bag in a unique brocade design with the Pylon and Sphere that represented the fair, with a brass frame and chain handle. 6.25 inches square. *Courtesy of Mary Efron, NYC.* No price available.

A fascinating collectible as well as a fun handbag.

Chapter Ten

Fun Future Collectibles

Black faille special occasion or evening handbag, with a single black leather top handle, with silver-tone buckles at each side, flap and snap closure, with black leather decorated with an elaborate starfish, encrusted with turquoise, marcasite, and diminutive Swarovski crystal, with a single compartment, lined with black faille, and one zippered pocket, gold-tone labeled *Ramon Tenza*, and a second black label with gold lettering, *Made In Spain*. 8 inches by 5.5 inches by 3.5 inches, 2005. *Courtesy of Judy A. Moyer*.

You can't go wrong buying beautifully crafted, high-end handbags with unusual design motifs.

Fuzzy white faux fur pouch handbag, with double top handles of gold leather and gold-tone chains through two sets of grommets, with a snap closure, single compartment with one zippered and one gathered pocket, lined with black taffeta, labeled *Fashion Express*. 10 inches by 6.5 inches by 4.5 inches, 2005. *Author's collection*.

Reminiscent of a vintage 1940s muff, this frivolous, fun handbag elicits comment wherever it goes.

Small cylindrical, shiny plastic handbag, with images of tiny license plates for various states, including "New York, Love NYC, The Empire State;" "Alaska Big Bear, The Last Frontier;" "Florida, Sunshine State;" "Hawaii, Hula23;" and others. Shiny iridescent blue plastic ends, a snap clasp styled with a rhinestone-decorated bottle cap and iridescent pale blue leather strap, single iridescent pale blue leather top handle, additional narrow iridescent pale blue shoulder strap, and single compartment lined with pale blue velour, labeled *Prezzo, A Division of Y & S Handbags, Inc*. 4.25 inches by 4 inches. 2005. *Author's collection*.

How could you not love this silly little handbag?

ALOHA STATE
HOLLYWOOD
NEW YORK
ALASKA
BIG BEAR
The Last Frontier
FLORIDA
SUN
TEX
NYC
ANNA NADLER

Iridescent taupe leather special occasion handbag, with a unique, handcrafted clasp of nickel decorated with red coral, attached to the 24-inch shoulder strap, lifting from the top of the handbag to reveal a snap closure and a single compartment, lined with black silk, labeled *Kemango, Hecho En Mexico*. 8.5 inches by 5.5 inches by 2.5 inches, 2005. *Author's collection, a gift from Judy A. Moyer*.

A unique and artistically crafted jewel!

Fuchsia suede and reptile-embossed leather corset handbag, with double reptile-embossed top handles, fuchsia satin ribbon laces through silver-tone grommets, a fuchsia satin bow and silver-tone filigreed heart, zippered closure, single compartment with one zippered pocket, lined with fuchsia cotton, labeled *Sonoma life + style For Her*. 8.5 inches by 6.5 inches by 3.5 inches, 2005. *Author's collection, a gift from Tara L. Flynn*.

This bright little corset handbag is for the fashion courageous! Like the handbag lamps, corset handbags had a short run in the retail marketplace, which makes them serious contenders as future collectibles.

Small black Persian lamb muff bag, with a zippered compartment, lined with beige cotton flannel, actual muff lined with black crepe. 8 inches by 7 inches, 1940s. *Courtesy of Robert Browne*. $95 – 115.

This tiny muff is a great alternative to an evening pocketbook—and it will keep your hands warm.

Resources

The Internet is a marvelous resource. One of my favorite websites is Linda Ames' Vintage Textile (www.vintagetextile.com), which never fails to have some fascinating designer handbags for sale. I absolutely love enokiworld (www.enokiworld.com), a website with high-end vintage and designer clothing and accessories, including some fabulous handbags. Marion Spitzley, a.k.a. "The Bag Lady" has recently opened the Bag Lady University, with an archive of information about handbag designers and manufacturers, a great resource for collectors. Her website (www.bagladyemporium.com) has perhaps the most comprehensive offering of vintage handbags on the Internet. I also enjoy visiting "Miss Kitty" of The Cat's Pajamas (www.catspajams.com) to see what she has "on the catwalk."

Antique and vintage clothing shops and shows, multi-dealer antiques malls and markets, flea markets, rummage sales, consignment shops, and thrift shops are all excellent places to find vintage handbags.

Books relating to the history and design of handbags are very useful. Review the bibliographies of each book you read for additional sources. Pamela Smith's *Official Guide to Vintage Fashion And Fabrics* features extensive resources, including tips for Internet shopping, information about resale and consignment shops, and other valuable information for the collector.

Finally, auction houses are excellent sources of antique and vintage handbags from individual collections and estates.

Above:
Judy A. Moyer, who coordinates the antique and vintage clothing and accessories auctions at Alderfer Auction Company, Hatfield, Pennsylvania, holds a gold-tone kitten minaudiere by Judith Leiber, which sold at the November 17, 2005 auction. **$850 – 1500.**

Index

Note: Designers' names are alphabetized by first, then last names, as on their labels. Manufacturers and retail stores are alphabetized as designated on the handbags' labels.